German Sturmartillerie at War Vol.1

Text by Frank V. De Sisto
Color plates by Laurent Lecocq

German Spell Check: Ralph Zwilling
Copyright © 2008
by CONCORD PUBLICATIONS CO.
10/F, B1, 603-609 Castle Peak Road
Kong Nam Industrial Building
Tsuen Wan, New Territories
Hong Kong
www.concord-publications.com

All rights reserved. No part of
this publication may be reproduced,
stored in a retrieval system or
transmitted in any form or by any
means, electronic, mechanical,
photocopying or otherwise, without
the prior written permission of
Concord Publications Co.

We welcome authors who can help
expand our range of books. If you
would like to submit material,
please feel free to contact us.

We are always on the look-out for new,
unpublished photos for this series.
If you have photos or slides or
information you feel may be useful to
future volumes, please send them to us
for possible future publication.
Full photo credits will be given upon
publication.

ISBN 962-361-652-X
printed in Hong Kong

INTRODUCTION

Concept and Development of the Sturmgeschütz

Originally designed to meet the conceptual requirements of Erich von Manstein as set forth in 1936, the Sturmgeschütz III series proved itself to be an immensely successful infantry-support weapons system. Contrary to popular belief, it was not only initially conceived as Begleitartillerie (escort artillery) to accompany the infantry in the assault, but also as their prime means of mobile and protected defense against enemy tanks. Indeed, this is borne out by the original designation of the vehicle as the Pz.Sfl.III (s.PaK). In addition, its main armament, the 7.5cm Sturmkanone L/24 was a flat-trajectory gun, based upon that mounted on the Pz.Kpfw.IV medium tank; it was not a low-velocity howitzer.

Tactically, von Manstein envisioned that the Sturmgeschütz III would be attached directly to the Infanterie-Division in at least Abteilung (battalion) strength. He also insisted that the Sturmgeschütz III was not to be answerable to the Panzertruppen (armored troops). The Sturmgeschütz III was to work closely with the infantry to help in reducing enemy strong-points and machine-gun nests. Carrying a gun that was superior in armor penetration to the standard infantry anti-tank gun (the 3.7cm PaK35/36), the Sturmgeschütz III was also to be their primary means of defeating enemy armor.

It took the massive armored clashes on the Ostfront to fully prove the Sturmgeschütz III's worth as a potent tank-destroyer. That it was able to effectively keep pace with the threats it faced until the war's end was due more to the inherent soundness of the original concept and design, than to frantic efforts to play "catch up" in the classic gun vs. armor conflict.

Production

The Sturmgeschütz III was built in several Ausfuhrungen (models) as follows:

Sturmgeschütz III Ausf.A (Sd.Kfz.142)

The first production series saw 30 built on the 5/Z.W. (Pz.Kpfw.III Ausf.F) chassis. A second series of 20 more were built on the 6/Z.W. (Pz.Kpfw.III Ausf.G) chassis with an additional 20mm of armor bolted on the bow plate. The main external characteristics of the first series included the forward-most return roller on each side, mounted in the original position, with the first design of shock absorber (021 B 9209). The cast drive sprocket (021 B 92011) featured eight circular perforations around its rim. The road-wheels with 75mm-wide tires and the idler wheel (021 B 92011) were also of the original design, intended for use with 36cm track (Kgs 6110/380/120). It also had cube-shaped stowage lockers mounted on the rear of the track-guards. The second series retained the hull-side escape hatches of the Pz.Kpfw.III Ausf.G, as well as transmission access hatch lids that opened fore-to-aft.

Sturmgeschütz III Ausf.B (Sd.Kfz.142)

This was built in two series; the first saw 250 built, while the second saw 50 built, all on the 7/Z.W. (Pz.Kpfw.III Ausf.H) chassis. Compared to the Ausf.A, the roof flaps for the gunner's Sfl. Z.F. sight and the commander's Scherenfernrohr SF.14Z (scissors periscope) were slightly modified, while the front return roller was eventually moved forward; some time earlier, the stowage cubes were deleted from the track-guards.

Sturmgeschütz III Ausf.C (Sd.Kfz.142)

A relatively short production run of 50 of this model were built on the 7/Z.W. (Pz.Kpfw.III Ausf.H) chassis. The superstructure roof layout was changed to include an opening for the gunner's new Sfl. Z.F.1 sight. Changes to the front of the casemate, included the deletion of the "tunnel" and opening for the original gunner's sight as seen on the StuG.III Ausf.A and Ausf.B. A new cast drive sprocket (021 B 39008) was introduced along with 40cm tracks (Kgs 61/40/120), a new idler wheel (021 B 39004) and a new shock absorber unit (021 B 39006); the road-wheels (021 B 9205) had their tires widened from 75mm to 95mm.

Sturmgeschütz III Ausf.D (Sd.Kfz.142)

Essentially what would be termed a "contract extension", the 150 Ausf.Ds built were externally the same as the previous StuG.III Ausf.C, except for changes in the engine deck hatch lids to improve cooling. The Ausf.D continued to be based on the 7/Z.W. (Pz.Kpfw.III Ausf.H) chassis.

Sturmgeschütz III Ausf.E (Sd.Kfz.142)

Of the 500 Ausf.Es ordered, 284 were built with the 7.5cm StuK L/24; the rest were completed as Ausf.Fs with the 7.5cm StuK40 L/43 and L/48; these were based on the 7/Z.W. (Pz.Kpfw.III Ausf.H) chassis. A new armored radio pannier was added to the right side of the superstructure, while on the left side, the existing pannier was lengthened.

Sturmgeschütz III Ausf.F (Sd.Kfz.142)

The first 120 built Ausf.Fs were fitted with the new 7.5cm StuK40 L/43, with a further 246 fitted with the StuK40 L/48. This model featured a redesigned roof plate with raised center section, which mounted a new fume extractor fan cover; it was based on the 7/Z.W. (Pz.Kpfw.III Ausf.H) chassis. The installation of the 7.5cm StuK40 necessitated the design of a new slab-sided, welded gun mantle.

Sturmgeschütz III Ausf.F/8 (Sd.Kfz.142)

A further 250 Ausf.F/8s were built on the newest available chassis, the 8/Z.W. (Pz.Kpfw.III Ausf.J). Although Ausf.F/8s were essentially the same as the previous StuG.III Ausf.F, external differences introduced on the 8/Z.W. chassis included the new hull rear armor plate layout; the forward upper corners of the hull side plates were extended and drilled as tow shackles, replacing the previous castings that were bolted to the glacis plate.

Sturmgeschütz III Ausf.G (Sd.Kfz.142/1)

Approximately 7,800 of the penultimate version of the StuG.III were built on the 8/Z.W. (Pz.Kpfw.III Ausf.J) chassis. Production began in December of 1942 and continued until the end of the war, with many major and minor changes to the vehicle's external appearance.

The initial version of the Ausf.G had a new hatch lid arrangement for the loader, a new commander's cupola on the roof plate and a slot for the gunner's sight; it retained the vent cover on the roof plate (without the vertically extended roof section as seen on the previous the StuG.III Ausf.F and F/8) and had a completely re-designed casemate, featuring integral panniers with rearward-angled front plates. It retained the driver's binocular periscopes, and initially had a vision flap, then an MP-Stopfen (pistol port) to left of the driver.

30mm Zusatzpanzer (appliqué armor) plates were bolted to the hull front, glacis plate and casemate front plates. The latter location featured a space between the plates where the driver's periscope openings were seen, and is a simple visual means of recognizing the type.

The next version of the StuG.III Ausf.G moved the vent cover from the roof plate to the rear of the casemate, added a sliding armored cover to the roof-mounted gunner's sight opening and introduced a hinged shield for the loader's external MG. The angle of the armor plate on the front of the casemate panniers was made steeper, the driver's periscopes were deleted, as well as the pistol port to the his left. Mounts and frames for Schürzen plates (side skirts) were introduced to counter Soviet infantry anti-tank rifles, which at close range could penetrate the hull sides. In September 1943, a coating of Zimmerit (a concrete-like paste) was applied to the vertical surfaces of the vehicle; this was introduced to combat the perceived threat of magnetic anti-tank grenades and mines. The Alkett factory applied Zimmerit in a pattern that has become known as the "waffle" style, while the MIAG pattern consisted of cross-hatching. Triple Nebelwurfgerät (smoke candle launchers) were sometimes fitted to each forward corner of the casemate.

Incremental changes included a cast Topfblende (pot-handle) gun mantle (supplementing, but not superceding the welded version), a cast armored deflector shield covering the frontal aspect of the commander's cupola, and the introduction of 80mm front plates on the hull, glacis and starboard front casemate plate. In addition, three types of all-steel return rollers (one had six ribs radiating from the hub, another had six perforations around its rim and the third combined these features) were gradually introduced as a measure to conserve rubber; Zimmerit was discontinued in September 1944.

The final production versions had a revised loader's hatch arrangement (changed from hinging fore-to-aft, to side-to-side), a Rundumfeuer (360-degree rotating remote-control MG34) with shields, a Nahverteidigunswaffe (close defense weapon) and a co-axial MG34 mounted alongside the StuK40; the latter was fitted to both the cast and welded mantles. Some had a factory-installed stowage rack on the engine deck and revised spare road-wheel stowage.

A small production series of StuG.III Ausf.G was built on the 10/Z.W. (Pz.Kpfw.III Ausf.M) chassis. These vehicles mounted the standard deep-fording exhaust pipe and muffler arrangement as well as the one-piece, forward-hinging glacis plate access hatch lids specific to that chassis.

Sturmhaubitze Ausf.G (Sd.Kfz.142/2)
Twelve pre-production Sturmhaubitze were constructed on re-built StuG.III chassis, most of which were eventually sent to the Ostfront. Later, approximately 1,300 vehicles were built on the StuG.III Ausf.G chassis. This type mounted a version of the standard divisional light howitzer, the 10.5cm l.FH18M. When fitted to the vehicle it was termed as the 10.5cm StuH42; 36 rounds were stowed to serve the howitzer. Three types of muzzle brakes were fitted, while some vehicles were seen with none at all. In other respects, the same changes seen on the standard StuG.III Ausf.G throughout its production life could be seen on the Sturmhaubitze.

Sturmgeschütz III Ausf.G Described
The StuG.III Ausf.G was the ultimate production model of this very effective German WW2 assault gun. It was the most widely produced model of the entire Sturmgeschütz series and continued in production from December 1942 until the war's end, first by Alkett and eventually also by MAN and MIAG.

The vehicle weighed in at 23.9 metric tons, was 6.77 meters long, 2.95 meters wide and 2.16 meters high, overall. It was powered by a Maybach HL120 TRM V-12 gasoline engine, which developed 265 horsepower. The S.S.G. transmission had six forward and one reverse gear and allowed the vehicle a top road speed of 40km. per hour on roads. Range on roads was 155km.

The four-man crew (commander, driver, gunner and radio operator/loader) was provided with a Fu 15 or 16, plus an intercom; additional radios could be installed to produce a command vehicle. Aside from their personal side arms, there was also an MP38 or MP40 stowed internally for the use of the crew.

The main armament was the 7.5cm StuK.40 L/48, which was supplied with 54 rounds of ammunition. This gun could penetrate up to 143mm (at 30-degrees) of armor at 100 meters, down to 77mm at 1,500 meters, with the Pzgr.40 armor-piercing round; in theory it could penetrate the frontal armor of most Allied and Soviet tanks at so-called "normal" battle ranges. Secondary armament eventually comprised of an MG34 or 42, fired by the loader from his open hatch. Later, the MG34 was mounted in the Rundumfeuer (360-degree rotating remote-control mount) with shields, and a Nahverteidigunswaffe (close defense weapon) was fitted to the casemate roof plate. Finally, a co-axial MG34 was mounted alongside the StuK40 on very late types.

Unit Organization
As initially deployed, each Sturmgeschütz-Batterien (roughly the size of a company) was assigned to a higher unit for command and control purposes. Later, larger units of Abteilung (battalion) strength were created; some were given Brigade status when a Begleit-Kompanie (infantry escort company) was attached.

The initial series of Ausf.As served in France with Sturmgeschütz-Batterien 640, 659, 660 and 665, which were formed with six assault guns per Batterie in accordance with Kriegsstarkenachweisungen (organizational table) K.St.N.445, as of November 1, 1939. A Batterie attached to the SS formation, Leibstandarte Adolf Hitler, was in training and saw no action in that campaign. The second production series of Ausf.As were issued to Sturmgeschütz-Batterien 666 and 667, too late to see combat in France.

Typical for any military organization, the structure of the Sturmgeschütz Abtielungen underwent periodic changes. Authorized 7 StuG.IIIs per Batterie according to K.St.N.446 (dated 18 April, and 1 November, 1941), this structure allowed for the Batterie Kommandeur (battery commander) to have his own assault gun. When Sturmgeschütz-Abteilungen were formed from three Batterien, there were 21 guns in such a unit.

A new series of K.St.N. charts were issued on 1 November 1942. Under K.St.N.446a, the units were authorized 10 Sturmgeschütze for each of the three Batterien within the Abteilung. Notably, this is the first time that the Abteilung Kommandeur (battalion commander) was officially allotted his own Sturmgeschütz, giving a total of 31 guns per Abteilung. Previously he had commanded from a Liechter Gepanzerter Beobachtungskraftwagen Sd.Kfz.253 (light armored observation vehicle). This was based on the Sd.Kfz.250-series of half-track, and in fact preceded it into production.

K.St.N.446b of February 1, 1944 authorized each Batterie to be reorganized with 14 Sturmgeschütze. Including the 3 Sturmgeschütz of the Abteilung Stabs (battalion headquarters), a Sturmgeschütz-Abteilung organized in this manner contained 45 Sturmgeschütze.

When Sturmhaubitze production reached its stride, Sturmgeschütz-Abteilungen with 10 guns per Batterie were authorized to have 3 Sturmhaubitze each. Those with 14 guns per Batterie were allotted 4 Sturmhaubitze.

The Sturmgeschütz III was frequently called upon to act as a surrogate Panzer when the Panzertruppen needed to fill out units, but no tanks were available. A Panzer-Sturmgeschütz-Kompanie organized as per K.St.N.1159, of June and November 1943 would contain 14 guns. A larger formation, organized as per K.St.N.1158 of April and November 1943, fielded 22 guns in each Panzer-Sturmgeschütz-Kompanie.

Infanterie-Divisionen normally had a Sturmgeschütz unit attached for support; these were not organic to the division. Since the type was considered to be successful, eventually the Infanterie-Divisionen clamored for their own organic Sturmgeschütz assets. Designated Sturmgeschütz-Panzer-Jäger-Kompanie, K.St.N.1149a allotted these units 10 guns; K.St.N.1149b gave them 14 guns.

A total of approximately 10,529 (or 10,304; sources differ) Sturmgeschütz IIIs and Sturmhaubitze were accepted by the Waffenamt from December 1939 through April 1945. Despite the obvious tactical handicap imposed by a limited-traverse main gun, the type proved eminently adaptable to evolving battlefield conditions; von Manstein's "offspring" can certainly claim to have been an extremely effective design.

Select Bibliography
There are lots of books devoted to German Sturmartillerie during World War Two. While this bibliography is far from complete, here is a listing of helpful published references and web-sites.

Sturmgeschütz, s.PaK to Sturmmörser, Panzer Tracts No.8, by T. Jentz & H. Doyle.
Panzerkampfwagen III, Ausf.E, F, G und H, Panzer Tracts No.3-2, by T. Jentz & H. Doyle.
Sturmgeschütz and its Variants, Speilberger Series Vol.II, Schiffer, by W. Spielberger.
Pz.Kpfw.III and its Variants, Speilberger Series Vol.III, Schiffer, by W. Spielberger.
Pz.Kpfw.IV and its Variants, Speilberger Series Vol.IV, Schiffer, by W. Spielberger.
Sturmgeschütz III Assault Gun 1940-42, Osprey New Vanguard 19, by T. Jentz & H. Doyle.
Sturmgeschütz III & IV 1942-45, Osprey New Vanguard 37, by T. Jentz & H. Doyle.
Sturmartillerie & Panzerjäger 1939-1945, Osprey New Vanguard 34, by B. Perrett.
The Sturmgeschütze in World War II 1939-1945, a Photo Chronicle, Schiffer, by W. Fleischer & R. Eiermann.
Sturmgeschütz Vor!, J.J. Fedorowicz, by F. Kurowski.
7,000 Kilometers in a Sturmgeschütz, J.J. Fedorowicz, by H. Engel.
Encyclopedia of German Tanks of World War Two, Revised Edition, by P. Chamberlain, H. Doyle & T. Jentz.
Sturmgeschütz III, Squadron Armor in Action 14, by B. Culver.
Sturmgeschütz III Ausf.G, Squadron Walk Around 5702, by T. Cockle.
Sturmartillerie, Aero Armor 3, by W. Spielberger & U. Feist.
StuG.III, Sturm & Drang 2.
Sturmgeschütz III, StuG.IV & s.IG33, Achtung Panzer 5, by M. Bitoh, H. Kitamura, T. Namie & S. Hards.
Sturmgeschütz III in Kampfeinsatz, Tankograd 4007, by M. Zöllner.
Sturmtiger, Wydawnictwo Militaria 188, by J. Ledwoch.
StuG w Akcji, Armagedon, by A. Majewski.
Sturmpanzer IV Brummbär, Kagerao Photosniper 12, by G. Parada & K. Mucha.
Sd.Kfz.166 Sturmpanzer Brummbär Vol.1, J.J. Fedorowicz, by W. Trojca & M. Jaugitz.
StuG.III w Miniaturie, Kagero 35001, by G. Parada & S. Jablonski.
Sturmgeschütz III, Miltar's Kits Hors Serie 3, by V. Deygas & A. Milesi.
Modelling the Sturmgeschütz III, Osprey Modelling 22, by G. Edmundson.
World War II Day By Day, wwiidaybyday.com, by Christoph Awender.
Die Sturmartillerie, www.die-sturmartillerie.com, by Florian Aufsess.

The author acknowledges his debt to these researchers, authors, artists, webmasters and modelers for their work relating to the history of this fascinating aspect of Germany's World War Two use of armored fighting vehicles. Any errors of fact or interpretation are my responsibility.

Additionally, my thanks go to my partner in these two books, Laurent Lecocq for his wonderful color plates and to Freddie Leung and the team at Concord for uncovering so many new and interesting photographs.

A Note on the Photographs
The photographs that appear in these two volumes came from a variety of sources. While every attempt was made to obtain fresh new images, some compromises had to be made. Therefore, in order to make the story as comprehensive as possible, within the limits of this series' format, previously-used images have been incorporated. Some of these images have been seen in my earlier Concord books, in particular the "Panzer Vor!" series. I have chosen to carry-over the captions that accompanied some of these images as well. Where necessary, corrections to those captions have been made.

Seen here with military men from several nations, the so-called "Father of the Sturmgeschütz", Generalfeldmarschall Erich von Manstein (at right, in side-cap) views a demonstration. Von Manstein was considered to be one of the best tacticians in the Deutsches Heer and was a successful field commander (for a time) on the Ostfront; he wears the shield commemorating his conquest of the Crimea on his left sleeve. He promulgated the concepts that led to the design, production and fielding of the Sturmgeschütz III.

The Sturmgeschütz III first saw combat service with several independent Sturmgeschütze-Batterien during the French Campaign of 1940. These two photographs depict Ausf.As entering a border crossing point during that campaign. These assault guns are identified as Ausf.As by the narrow 36cm tracks, and their associated road-wheels and drive sprocket. The spacing of the forward-most return rollers identifies these as Ausf.As. Although the cube-shaped stowage boxes on the track guards were a feature of the Ausf.A, they could also be seen on a few Ausf.Bs as well.

This rear view shows several interesting additions to a Sturmgeschütz III Ausf.A. Identified as an Ausf.A by the 36cm track, relatively evenly-spaced return rollers, narrow drive sprocket and road-wheels, it features a retro-fitted night-driving distance-keeping tail lamp. It also mounts a Nebelkerzenabwurfvorrichtung (rack to deploy smoke candles) in the un-armored configuration. Note also the lack of a rod antenna storage trough and the stowage cubes. The crewmen still wear their padded berets, suggesting this photograph was taken between the end of the French Campaign and the start of Operation Barbarossa.

A pair of Sturmgeschütz III Ausf.A leads an Opel Blitz 3-ton truck along a French road, during the 1940 campaign. The front assault gun is marked as being from Sturmgeschütz-Batterie 660, as denoted by the white-outline Maltese cross on the far mud-flap.

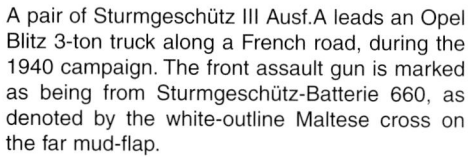

In this photo, an attempt is being made to clean a Stug.III Ausf.A. Note the way the roof is covered with a tarp and the relatively large, white-outline Balkenkreuz on the superstructure side spaced armor panel. The assault gun has the earlier narrow 36cm tracks as well as the narrow road-wheels. This photograph provides an excellent view of some of the vehicle's fittings such as the tow shackles, mud-flap hinges, horn, head-lamp and marker-lamp. Note also the tool box just behind the marker-lamp, and how it is mounted in an elevated position over other tools. This assault gun has been misidentified previously as an Ausf.B by this author.

This photograph shows a very rare sub-type of the equally rare StuG.III Ausf.A. It belongs to the second production batch of 20 vehicles, which were derived from Pz.Kpfw.III Ausf.G chassis. It is identified as such by the chassis number on the lower glacis plate, 90403. Other identifying features of this variant are the configuration of the hatch hinges on the upper glacis plate as well as the bolted-on armor on the lower glacis plate. These assault guns saw service after the end of the French Campaign and would have been finished in a solid covering of dunkelgrau RAL 7028. Note the presence of a Notek black-out driving head-lamp, which also would date this photo as post-June 1940. The officer in front of the StuG wears his trousers bloused over his boots, while the Hauptwachtmeister to the left wears his boots in the standard fashion with breeches tucked in; note the cuff-bands on both of his sleeves.

Too late to see combat during the 1940 French Campaign, the Waffen-SS had a single Batterie composed of Sturmgeschütz III Ausf.A, one of which is seen here during the opening stages of Operation Barbarossa. It is identified as an Ausf.A by the spacing of the forward-most return roller and the cube-shaped storage box on the track guards. Note the unit insignia from 4.(Sturmgeschütz) Kompanie bei V.(schweren) Bataillon Leibstandarte Adolf Hitler; it has often been depicted as a dog's head, but recent research has shown that it is actually a white eagle's head with the letters "LAH" superimposed on the neck. This in turn sits over a stylized yellow flame in the shape of an "S". This is thought to be the initial of the unit commander's last name, SS-Hauptsturmführer Georg Schönberger. Note that the Panzerjäger I Ausf.Bs in the background also have this insignia on their superstructure armor shields.

This Sturmgeschütz III Ausf.A is seen fitted with extra tracks on its front end for added protection. This was not often seen in the 1940 campaign, suggesting this image was created during the early part of Operation Barbarossa in 1941. Note that the infantrymen are huddled in the lee of the assault gun for protection and that the crewmen wear their steel helmets for additional protection. The spacing of the front return roller identifies this as an Ausf.A.

This Sturmgeschütz III can be identified as an Ausf.A by the location and configuration of the two small hatch lids forward of the commander's opened hatch lids. These differed slightly from the Ausf.A to Ausf.B. Note that the crew has added extra stowage items in the form of a locker on the starboard side track guard and spare track on the port side. The two wooden crates on the engine deck appear to be left-over 7.5cm StuK ammunition containers. Note that this assault gun does not have a stowage trough for the rod antenna; apparently, this was common on these early models.

While a group of infantrymen file past, this Sturmgeschütz III (either an Ausf.A or Ausf.B) stands idle in the shadow of a building. The lightweight marching order of the infantrymen and the attitude of the crew suggest this image was shot while the men are on a training exercise. The nearest person in the photograph is blocking the suspension details, making it impossible to know if the assault gun is an Ausf.A or Ausf.B; however, the location and style of the gunner's sight aperture confirms that it can only be one of these two models.

This Sturmgeschütz III Ausf.B is posing in front of its garage at the Kaserne of Artilleriem-Lehr-Regiment, Jüterbog. It wears the school insignia on the track guard's mud-flap as well as on the driver's armor plate; a gun-in-battery letter, "A", is seen on the off-side plate. This is identified as an Ausf.B by the location of the forward-most return roller, which was moved forward to prevent the newer wider track from striking the shock absorber (behind the drive sprocket, at this angle). It has wider 40cm tracks which necessitated a spacer ring for the drive sprocket. Note also that it still mounts a cube-shaped stowage locker on the rear of the track guards; these could also be seen on the Ausf.B.

A group of soldiers goes for a joyride on this Sturmgeschütz III Ausf.B. The assault gun is fitted with wider 40cm tracks; the relocated return roller and the shape of the armor in front of the gunner's sight identify this model.

These two photographs probably depict the same Sturmgeschütz III (Tac number 24), which may be an Ausf.B. Note that in one photograph, the accompanying infantrymen wear their fatigue trousers with their normal tunic, weapons and equipment, while one man on the assault gun has a white cloth band on his side-cap; this is a strong indication that these men are conducting a training exercise. Note also that the Sturmgeschütz crewman wears the padded beret in the field grey color typical of members of the Sturmartillerietruppen. In the second photo we see the assault gun moving at high speed; in this instance the crewmen wear the more widely-seen side-caps. Note the leichte Zugkraftwagen 1-ton Sd.Kfz.10 pulling a 3.7cm PaK35/36 in the background.

A Sturmgeschütz III Ausf.B lurks in a snow-covered wood, while its commander stands "head-out" of his hatch opening. Sections of small trees have been laid upon the front of the assault gun, while its relatively pristine condition suggests that this photograph was taken while on a training exercise, possibly during the winter of 1940-41.

About all that can be said as far as the model identification of this Sturmgeschütz III is that it is an Ausf.B, C, D or E. It has the return roller spacing introduced with the Ausf.B as well as the drive sprocket introduced during the production of that model. The remainder of the assault gun is covered with local foliage to help hide it from prying enemy eyes, thus making it impossible to determine the specific model.

A pair of Sturmgeschütz IIIs, led by an Ausf.B, travels down a dusty Soviet road some time during the opening phases of Operation Barbarossa. The near assault gun has the gunner's sight aperture in the configuration seen on the Ausf.B, as well as the refined suspension system. In the left foreground is what appears to be a command pennant, mounted on a thin rod.

Although difficult to say with any certainty, this Sturmgeschütz III is probably an Ausf.B; note how the canvas cover sags in the area that would house the "tunnel" that led to the gunner's sight aperture. This assault gun has suspension system attributes of the Ausf.B and also has the Notek black-out driving headlamp mounted on the near-side track guard. The crew has also mounted a length of spare track for extra protection, strung between the tow shackles at the bow.

This Sturmgeschütz III Ausf.B crosses a shallow river during the beginning of Operation Barbarossa in 1941. Note the position of the gun-in-battery letters and the small ring on the near-side mud-flap; there is also a white edge on the mud-flap to aid in low-light driving. This Ausf.B has the later drive sprocket, 40cm tracks and the re-located forward-most return roller.

This Sturmgeschütz III Ausf.B is marked as belonging to StuG.Abt.192, which saw combat on the Ostfront in 1941. It is identified as an Ausf.B by the configuration and location of the gunner's sight aperture and by the spacing of the return rollers. It wears 40cm tracks and mounts the newer drive sprocket introduced during Ausf.B production. This experienced crew has mounted a large wooden un-ditching beam on the starboard track guard, which was a common fitting of this unit. The crew has also added some extra protection to the bow by stringing a section of spare track from between the tow shackles. Note that the armored guard is missing from the starboard side head-lamp, which itself appears to have been damaged.

While a local peasant woman goes about her business, a pair of Sturmgeschütz III Ausf.Bs is attended to by their crews. Both assault guns wear the fairly deteriorated remnants of a winter white-wash camouflage finish; both also have "Winterketten" (winter tracks) fitted for better floatation in snow and mud. Note the spare road-wheel stored on the track guard and the tow cable in the "ready position" in case it is needed.

This crew has "broken track" on their Sturmgeschütz III Ausf.B during what is possibly the first frigid winter on the Ostfront. The assault gun has been given a coat of white-wash to conceal it against the snowy background. The crew has also placed spare track lengths on the side of the hull, no doubt having been made aware of the Soviet troops' anti-tank rifles' ability to penetrate the thin armor at relatively close ranges. Later, Schürzen (skirts) were fitted to many German Panzer and Sturmartillerie assets to combat this threat.

This ice- and snow-encrusted Sturmgeschütz III Ausf.B is attempting to pull a leichter Zugkraftwagen 3-ton Sd.Kfz.11 back onto a road, probably during the first winter on the Ostfront. The half-track is identified by the opening in the rear body panel, which was unique to the Sd.Kfz.11. Note the letters "BF" on the side of the assault gun; these possibly denoted this as the "Batterie-Führer's" mount.

In the midst of combat, this Sturmgeschütz III Ausf.B advances on an enemy position, its commander observing from under cover using his Scherenfernrohr (scissors periscope). This assault gun has been fitted with a Notek black-out head-lamp as well as the associated station-keeping tail-lamp. Note the large amount of gear stowed on the engine deck and the tow cable fixed to the rear hull plate, ready for instant use.

Although these infantrymen were lucky enough to be equipped with purpose designed snow-suits, one man's luck has taken a turn, since he has been wounded in his eye. They are accompanied by a Sturmgeschütz III Ausf.B, which is identified by the sight aperture for the gunner; it also wears a winter white-wash and mounts Winterketten (winter tracks).

A damaged Sturmgeschütz III Ausf.B sits on a railway flatcar, which is under tow by a schwere Zugkraftwagen 18-ton Sd.Kfz.9. The assault gun is marked with a white ring towards the rear of the Vorpanzer (spaced armor) plate, while a gun-in-battery letter ("E" or "F") is painted further forward on the casemate side.

The four-man crew of this Sturmgeschütz III (of an indeterminate model) poses in front of their mount; the uniforms of the men at far left and far right suggest that an award ceremony has taken place. The uniforms closely resembled those worn by Panzertruppen, but were issued in a Feldgrau (field grey) color; the thick Waffenfarbe (branch color) piping on their epaulettes suggest they are both NCOs. The two other men seem more concerned with keeping warm, rather than looking fashionable; one wears padded overalls, while the other wears his great-coat. The only unusual visible feature on the assault gun is the wire brush guard that protects the Notek black-out driving head-lamp.

A group of infantrymen take shelter behind a Sturmgeschütz III, of an indeterminate model. Note that many of the men are wearing low-cut lace-up boots with canvas gaiters and that some also carry an unusually large rolled cloth bundle on their harnesses. One of the soldiers has carelessly left a tripod in the wake of the vehicle's tracks; if it reverses suddenly, the equipment will be lost. Note the white-outline Balkenkreuz national insignia painted on the Nebelkerzenabwurfvorrichtung (rack to deploy smoke candles) as well as the insignia of an unidentified unit on the starboard mud-flap.

This Sturmgeschütz III Ausf.C/D raises a tactically un-sound cloud of dust as it moves at speed over a dusty Russian road. The configuration of the forward upper armor plates on the casemate is indicative of the Ausf.C and D, which were nearly identical externally. This assault gun has the return roller spacing introduced on the StuG.III Ausf.B, as well as new drive sprocket and idler wheels, introduced on the Ausf.C.

Although it only shows a part of a Sturmgeschütz III (possibly an Ausf.B), this photograph is full of interesting details. Foremost among them is the unit insignia of StuG.Abt.184, a hand grasping a sword, on a background of flame, with the motto "Ferro Ignique" beneath. Some interesting details of the assault gun's commander's M1940 tunic can also be noted, including the ribbon in his lapel for the Iron Cross 2nd class, what appears to be a Wound Badge on his breast, and his officer's style leather belt. As he shouts an order, one can also note that he's wearing a steel helmet and has binoculars hung from his neck. Details of the flexible rubber base for the rod antenna can be seen as well as the Scherenfernrohr (scissors periscope).

A column of six Sturmgeschütz IIIs pauses during the advance into the Soviet Union during the early stages of Operation Barbarossa. The first assault gun is an Ausf.B; the cut-out in front of the gunner's Sfl.Z.F. sight can be seen at the edge of the original photograph. It is followed by an Ausf.C/D with Sfl.Z.F.1 gun sight and modified superstructure plate in front of it; note also the revised configuration of the superstructure on the starboard side, above the skull-and-crossbones insignia of StuG.Abt.192. Compare the superstructure to the following assault guns, all of which are Ausf.Bs.

The carcass of a Sturmgeschütz III Ausf.C/D receives the attention of several infantrymen. Note the gun-in-battery marking ("A", for "Anton") as well as the white-outline Balkenkreuz on the track guard-mounted armored pannier; there also appears to be another obscured marking, just forward of the national insignia. Since much of the track guards have been torn away, the modeler is provided with a rare view of the scalloped flange that was welded to the hull side walls, especially towards the vehicle's rear. This was drilled for bolts, which were used to attach the engine deck and superstructure to the hull; these could in turn be removed so that either could be lifted away for maintenance or an engine change.

Moving at speed and therefore resulting in a blurred image, this Sturmgeschütz III Ausf.C/D exhibits the main external features introduced on this type. It features the new drive sprocket and idler wheel and the associated wider 40cm track, as well as the later return roller spacing. The casemate front has been reconfigured, with the gunner's sight tunnel eliminated when the sight was re-located to protrude only from the roof plate. This assault gun has a Notek black-out head-lamp on the near-side track guard and a tarp laid over the casemate roof to keep out the elements.

Parked on a typical Russian "road" this Sturmgeschütz III Ausf.C/D is surrounded by the litter of war; note the burnt-out Soviet truck in the foreground.

Infantrymen mount a StuG.III Ausf.C/D, which is being used as a "battle taxi" to ferry the men to their next action. The lead assault gun is identified as an Ausf.C/D by the configuration of the superstructure plate in front of the gunner's Sfl.Z.F.1 sight; it no longer has the "tunnel" with baffles since the sight now protrudes from the roof of the casemate. Note that the opposite side of the superstructure has been re-configured as well; compare it to the layout of any StuG.III Ausf.B previously shown.

It would appear that the crew of this Sturmgeschütz III Ausf.C or D is repainting their assault gun with fresh Dunkelgrau paint, possibly in the spring of 1942. Note the fresh paint on the drive sprocket and the remains of what appears to be a winter white-wash on the two forward-most road-wheels. All "soft gear" (such as crew's personal belongings and tarps) has been removed, with spare track sections and road-wheels left in place for the new paint job. Some units stored spare torsion bars on the hull side walls, which may explain the rod-like item seen below the return rollers. This Sturmgeschütz III is identified as an Ausf.C or D by the configuration of the casemate front as well as by the later drive sprocket and idler wheel; of course the latter two items were commonly retro-fitted to remaining Ausf.Bs as well.

This Sturmgeschütz III Ausf.C or D leads a column of halftracks including a leichte Gepanzerte Munitionskraftwagen Sd.Kfz.252 (light armored ammunition transporter) with trailer. It would appear that the second halftrack is also an Sd.Kfz.252. The final vehicle may be either another '252 or a leichte Gepanzerte Beobachtungskraftwagen Sd.Kfz.253 (light armored observation). As initially organized, Sturmgeschütz-Batterien were equipped with both types of halftracks. This assault gun is identified as an Ausf.C or D by the shape of the front of the casemate. The later Ausf.E would have had an armored radio pannier fitted over the track guard on the starboard side (visible in this photo), which is not seen here.

Intent upon saving their battered feet, a group of German infantrymen attempt to crank-start their captured Soviet truck, while a Sturmgeschütz III lingers in the background. The assault gun has the later drive sprocket introduced with the Ausf.C, but otherwise cannot be positively identified as a specific model at this angle and distance.

A Pz.Kpfw.III Ausf.J is attempting to free a snow-bound Sturmgeschütz III Ausf.E using a tow cable. The Pz.Kpfw.III is identified as an Ausf.J by the configuration of the 50mm-thick superstructure front plate and the extended hull side plates that were drilled to serve as towing brackets; it mounts a short 5cm KwK. The Sturmgeschütz III is identified as an Ausf.E by the new armored radio pannier that was added to the starboard-side track guard; compare this image to the previous image of an Ausf.C/D. This assault gun has been whitewashed for concealment against the snow and there is an undecipherable name painted on the pannier side.

This Sturmgeschütz III (possibly an Ausf.E) has been disarmed and is serving as a driver training vehicle; note the partially obscured painted-on plate on the bow, which reads "Fahrschule" (driver's school). It has been re-painted in the later war base color of Dunkelgelb, and retrofitted with a Notek black-out driving headlamp on the glacis plate.

A column of assault guns stretches off to the horizon as German forces mass for an attack. The near Sturmgeschütz III is an Ausf.E as evidenced by the armored pannier over the near fender and the lack of the angled supplementary armor plate seen forward of it on the earlier Ausf.B. The near assault gun is also fitted out as a command vehicle, as is evidenced by the rod antennae at both corners of the casemate rear. The armored pannier is marked with a white-outline Balkenkreuz national insignia (another is on the engine deck rear plate), with an undecipherable name just forward of it. In addition, each gun is transporting a number of infantrymen, a sure sign of impending action.

A German infantryman, armed with a captured Soviet Tokarev SVT-40 semi-automatic rifle crouches under cover of foliage with his comrades, while a Sturmgeschütz III Ausf.E creeps forward. Identified as an Ausf.E by the armored radio pannier over the near-side track guard, this assault gun is marked with a white "A" (for "Anton"), which is its gun-in-battery designator. A standardized black/white Balkenkreuz is positioned after the "A", while it appears that a two-tone camouflage pattern has been applied.

More infantrymen move towards the front accompanied by a column of German AFVs. The leading element in the column is a Sturmgeschütz III Ausf.B as shown by the configuration of the gunner's sight aperture. Behind it is an armored half-track, possibly the associated Sd.Kfz.252 or Sd.Kfz.253. The former was configured as a leichte Gepanzerte Munitionskraftwagen. (light armored ammunition transporter) while the latter was configured as a leichte Gepanzerte Beobachtungskraftwagen (light armored observation vehicle).

One infantryman grabs onto the bore swab staffs preparatory to climbing on board this Sturmgeschütz III Ausf.B, as an MG34 team makes themselves comfortable on the engine deck. This photograph amply demonstrates the symbiotic relationship that initially existed between the two arms. The assault gun supported the infantry by reducing enemy strong-points and combating enemy armor, while the infantry protected the assault guns from enemy close-range anti-armor assets.

A Sturmgeschütz III Ausf.B, accompanied by infantry, passes through a recently shot-up vehicle column. Since the assault guns are headed in a direction opposite the burning column, it can be surmised that these were once functioning enemy assets. Perhaps they were surprised when the German AFVs topped the crest of the ridge in the distance? This dusty Ausf.B is identified by the configuration of the area around the gunner's sight aperture.

The commander of this Sturmgeschütz III Ausf.B observes the fall of shot from his open hatch; note his Scherenfernrohr (scissors periscope) mounted in front of him, which he can use to observe from under armor. This Ausf.B has features typical of its type, such as later drive sprocket, wider 40cm tracks and return roller moved further forward. It also has what appear to be the stowage style and markings of an assault gun from StuG.Abt.192. Note the opened engine deck access hatch lid; this was commonly done to provide better engine cooling, especially during the first summer of that gargantuan campaign on the Ostfront.

While a couple of infantrymen "ride shotgun", the crew of this buttoned-down Sturmgeschütz III Ausf.B prepares to engage the enemy. Another item introduced during production of the Ausf.B was a new cast idler wheel, as seen here.

A group of infantrymen camp on the verge of a road (not a wise move since that area was designed specifically to help rain-water drain from the road; on the other hand, it may be tactically sound as it does provide some defilade from enemy fire and observation) as a pair of Sturmgeschütz III Ausf.Bs pass by. The near assault gun has stowage associated with StuG.Abt.192, specifically the large wood un-ditching beam on the near-side track guard.

This heavily-stowed, winter white-washed Sturmgeschütz III Ausf.E, moves forward in column formation. This assault gun wears the wider Winterketten (winter tracks) for better flotation in deep snow. Note the position of the stowed road-wheel, the configuration of the Balkenkreuz and how it is outlined with the white paint of the winter camouflage scheme.

A column of Sturmgeschütz III Ausf.Fs moves through a village on the Ostfront. The Ausf.F is identified by the StuK40 gun tube locked in travel position by an internal device; it protrudes forward, ahead of the first man seated on the casemate. Many Ausf.Fs were built on assault guns that were originally part of the Ausf.E contract and from the rear can be differentiated from the Ausf.F/8 by the configuration of the armor plate as seen here. This Ausf.F also has an armored Nebelkerzenabwurfvorrichtung (rack to deploy smoke candles) on the rear plate, with a typically-positioned black/white Balkenkreuz.

A rather haggard-looking crewman walks past the bow of a Sturmgeschütz III Ausf.F, which is identified as such by the configuration of the tow cable mounts. Note the addition of Zusatzpanzer (appliqué armor) to the glacis plate and the area around the driver's visor; typically another plate would be attached to the lower bow but it is not clear in this photo. The Notek black-out driving head-lamp is in the position it will occupy through the end of Ausf.G production.

This rear view of a Sturmgeschütz III Ausf.F clearly shows the easiest way to differentiate this model from the later Ausf.F/8 from this angle; it has the earlier superstructure/hull rear plate configuration seen up to the Pz.Kpfw.III Ausf.H. The Ausf.F/8 was based on the Pz.Kpfw.III Ausf.J hull. Other features peculiar to both the Ausf.F and F/8 are the raised section of the casemate roof upon which was mounted the cover for the crew compartment ventilation fan. This Sturmgeschütz mounts the long 7.5cm StuK40 with a cover over its muzzle brake.

Buried under foliage is a Sturmgeschütz III Ausf.F, as seen by the configuration of the tow shackles on the glacis plate. The StuK40 has been given special treatment to include a sheet or net, which completely disguises it. It also has its muzzle covered and the gun tube locked internally for travel.

Preceded by veteran MG42 machine-gun crew, a Sturmgeschütz III Ausf.F makes its way through some scrub-land. It is identified as an Ausf.F by the configuration of the cast and bolted tow shackles on the bow. Note the gun-in-battery letter, "F", on the casemate front and the multi-tone camouflage scheme. Its uncovered muzzle break suggests that action is either anticipated, or just completed; from the appearance of the infantrymen, it is quite probably the latter.

A scruffy Sturmgeschütz III Ausf.F passes through a small village, with the entire crew, except the driver, riding outside for some fresh air. These vehicles were supplied with a canvas foul weather cover, which, in this case is custom-fitted to the mantle of the StuK40. Note the welded Zusatzpanzer (appliqué armor) on the glacis plate and the area around the driver's visor; the plate on the bow is also recognizable due to the seam running between the two tow shackles.

Wearing the stylized "CH" insignia of StuG.Abt.210, this Sturmgeschütz III Ausf.F has been hidden in thick underbrush to keep it from prying enemy eyes. This assault gun is identified as an Ausf.F by the tow shackles seen on the bow; however, it appears not to have been fitted with Zusatzpanzer (appliqué armor) anywhere on its frontal arc.

Often, German factories were contracted in advance if a series of armored vehicles was destined for service in a warm or dusty climate. These were then built to Tropen (tropical) standards as seen here. This Sturmgeschütz III Ausf.F has had an air filter pre-cleaner mounted over the rear of the track guard, which is connected to the engine compartment by a pipe arrangement; it was also finished in a Tropen camouflage scheme, which at the time these assault guns were produced should have (officially) consisted of two colors: Braun RAL 8020 as the base with patches of Grau RAL 7027 covering remaining 1/3 of the vehicle. Note the Zusatzpanzer (appliqué armor) on the bow and glacis plates.

With most of a Batterie entrained somewhere on the Ostfront, the lead Sturmgeschütz III Ausf.F shows an unusual feature: it has had the armored headlamps and their covers removed, and what appears to be the mounting stalk for a Notek black-out head-lamp mounted on the center of the glacis plate. Further back on the train sits a leichte Gepanzerte Munitionskraftwagen Sd.Kfz.252 light armored ammunition transporter, identifiable by the acute angle of the superstructure armor and the opened hatch lid. This unit has also availed themselves of a captured Soviet STZ-5 artillery tractor, which no doubt came in quite handy considering local weather and topography.

The crew-members of this Sturmgeschütz III Ausf.B inspect their swamped assault gun, which sits in the middle of a Russian river; who gave the order that caused it to wind up in such a predicament is left un-recorded! This angle and the fact that the assault gun has recently been "washed" afford a clear view of some details, notably the hinge style on the transmission inspection hatch lids. Other items of note are the canvas cover on the casemate roof (installed to keep water out!) and the lack of any marker lamps; the conduits for them are still visible on each forward end of the track guards.

As bicycle-mounted infantrymen scurry along the verge of a road, a Sturmgeschütz III Ausf.B moves towards the front. The men in the foreground obscure much of the assault gun's features, but the tunnel in front of the gunner's sight aperture can just be seen behind the helmet of the man second from right. It would also appear that wider 40cm tracks have been installed.

A Sturmgeschütz III Ausf.B negotiates some rough, wooded terrain on the Ostfront. The commander is wearing his steel helmet, which suggests that combat is imminent. This assault gun has the later wider drive sprocket as well as wider 40cm track; the idler wheel id the original design. It wears the insignia of StuG.Abt.243.

This Sturmgeschütz III Ausf.B follows a companion vehicle across a pre-fabricated bridge. The near assault gun carries the cross-in-shield insignia of StuG.Abt.201, painted on the armored Nebelkerzenabwurfvorrichtung (rack to deploy smoke candles) mounted on the superstructure rear plate. At the left is a barely visible, dust-covered Balkenkreuz national insignia. Both assault guns are very heavily stowed with spare track sections and road-wheels. Typical at river crossing sites, there are loads of Pioniertruppen standing about, waiting as all soldiers do, for something to happen. In the second photograph, another Sturmgeschütz III Ausf.B from the same unit crosses the bridge, as seen by a photographer who has positioned himself down on the river itself.

This pair of unusually-marked Sturmgeschütz III Ausf.Fs lead a leichte Gepanzerte Munitionskraftwagen Sd.Kfz.252 light armored ammunition transporter, which itself is drawing an Sd.Ah.52 ammunition trailer. Note the tactical symbols for a tracked assault gun unit on the half-track and trailer, as well as the "WH"-prefixed registration plate on the former. The assault guns feature large unit-mounted stowage lockers on their rear decks, which are decorated with a Balkenkreuz, a Tac number and a colored bar. The near assault gun features white bars, while the far one wears blue, green or red bars; these colors generally denoted the specific Batterie within the Abteilung.

While a group of interested infantrymen look on, two Sturmgeschütz III Ausf.F/8s pull another Ausf.F/8 from a water obstacle, somewhere on the Ostfront. The assault gun nearest the camera has ice built up on its front end from its immersion, but it is clearly an F/8 as the earlier, larger tow shackle mounts are not in evidence. On the two further vehicles it is clear that they are also F/8s, since it can easily be seen that they have the extended hulls with drilled upper corners. The near assault gun has the earlier "globular" single-baffle muzzle brake on its StuK40, and shows the housing for the fighting compartment fume extractor fan on the superstructure roof between the commander's and loader's hatch lids. Also of interest is the way the winter white-wash has been applied leaving distinct, hard-edged squiggles of the base color showing, which in this case should be Dunkelgrau RAL 7021.

The crew of this Sturmgeschütz III, which is either an Ausf.F or F/8, pauses to smile for the photographer. There are no readily visible features that can be used to tell which specific model this assault gun happens to be. Note the canvas draped over the perennially leaky fighting compartment and the cover over the muzzle brake.

A pair of crewmen converse next to their Sturmgeschütz III, which is also either an Ausf.F or F/8; again, there are no readily visible features for use in identifying the specific model. This assault gun has a winter white-wash applied over what is probably a Tropen camouflage scheme. Note the relatively light base color around the black/white Balkenkreuz as well as around the stenciled black "C", which is the gun-in-battery letter for this particular vehicle.

A cloud of dust settles in front of this Sturmgeschütz III, which is either an Ausf.F or F/8. The features usually associated with this model can be seen including: raised section of the casemate roof upon which was mounted a dome for the crew compartment ventilation fan and the long 7.5cm StuK40 with the later double-baffle, bottle-shaped muzzle brake. This assault gun has extensive stowage including spare tracks and a road-wheel on the superstructure side as well as a rack with wooden stowage lockers on the rear deck.

This rather austere StuG.III Ausf.F/8 shows one of its most important identifying features: the hull side plate has been extended and drilled out to accept tow hooks. This Ausf.F/8 mounts a 7.5cm StuK40 L/48 with the double-baffle, bottle-shaped muzzle brake. Note also the pannier extension on the starboard side of the casemate, the rod and cap to store a spare road-wheel just forward of it and the Zusatzpanzerung (appliqué armor) mounted on both of the superstructure front plates. This Sturmgeschütz carries an unusual all-white Balkenkreuz national insignia on the pannier extension.

When constructed on the 8/Z.W. (Pz.Kpfw.III Ausf.J) chassis, the Sturmgeschütz III Ausf.F became the Ausf.F/8, as seen here. Note the configuration of the superstructure rear plate, which is the sure indicator from this angle. The engine deck has also been configured for Tropen (tropical) operation by having openings cut in the access hatch lids, which are in turn covered with cast armored cowls. This assault gun is also finished in the Tropen camouflage scheme and has a black/white Balkenkreuze painted directly on the spare track section seen on the superstructure side.

This pair of Sturmgeschütz III Ausf.F/8s show other features associated with this model. The glacis, bow and superstructure front plates of both are fitted with bolted-on 30mm-thick Zusatzpanzer (appliqué armor) plates. While more apparent on the far assault gun, both it, and the near one, mount Schürzen (skirts) to counter Soviet man-portable anti-tank rifles. The main feature distinguishing these Ausf.F/8s from the previous Ausf.F, from this angle, is the extended hull side plates, which have been drilled to accept tow hooks.

This Sturmgeschütz III Ausf.F/8 is flanked by an Ausf.G (at right) and an unidentified model (at left). This frontal view clearly shows the 30mm-thick welded Zusatzpanzer (appliqué armor) plates on the bow, glacis and superstructure front. The drilled out extended hull side plates identify this as an Ausf.F/8. Note also the spare track section on the bow, which features one link with a solid guide horn and the canvas protective cover on the muzzle brake.

A trio of assault guns, probably all Sturmgeschütz III Ausf.F/8s, is re-fueled from a Maultier (Mule) half-track. The insignia on the rear plate of the assault gun at far right is tentatively identified as belonging to StuG.Abt.244. Although most features are obscured, these are identified as Ausf.F/8 by the rear superstructure armor plate configuration and the apparent lack of a commander's cupola.

StuG.III Ausf.B, Artillerie-Lehr-Regiment, Jüterbog, Germany, possibly 1942
This training vehicle is possibly finished in one of the two "Tropen" schemes, the first of which was introduced in March of 1941. The base color was Gelbbraun RAL 8000, with patches of Graugrün RAL 7008 covering remaining 1/3 of the item. In March of 1942, this was changed to Braun RAL 8020 as the base with patches of Grau RAL 7027 covering remaining 1/3 of the item. A gun-in-battery letter, "A", appears on the starboard side superstructure front plate painted in red, while the school insignia, a red fish shape in a white wreath shape can be seen opposite; it is also repeated on the port side mud-flap. It is possible that the school insignia as well as the gun-in-battery letter were also repeated on the rear superstructure plate.

StuG.III Ausf.E, unidentified unit, Ostfront, 1942
Base painted in Dunkelgrau RAL 7021, this Ausf.E has been given a coat of whitewash leaving only the white Balkenkreuze visible, framed by an outline of the base color.

StuG.III Ausf.B, StuG.Abt.192, Ostfront, 1941
This vehicle is finished overall in Dunkelgrau RAL 7021. It is quite extensively marked, including a Tac number, white 33, on three sides of the superstructure. In addition, the unit's Death's Head insignia is seen in all three positions, near the Tac numbers. In this case, it is probably yellow on a black square. A white outline Balkenkreuz would also be seen forward on the superstructure side plates and on the port side of the rear plate. An oblong tactical sign with three vertical bars, painted in yellow, was seen on the glacis as well as the superstructure rear plate.

StuG.III Ausf.B, unidentified unit, Ostfront, 1941
Painted overall Dunkelgrau RAL 7021, this assault gun has a small white ring on the starboard rear mud-flap, as well as on the superstructure side plate; a similar device probably also appeared on the front starboard mud-flap. An oversized gun-in-battery letter, a white "B" is seen on the rear superstructure plate as well as on both sides of the casemate. Typically, these letters would also appear on the starboard front casemate plate. A large, thin, white outline Balkenkreuz was seen on both sides of the casemate.

StuG.III Ausf.B, unidentified unit, France, 1940-41
The two photographs upon which this plate is based show the vehicle during training, probably in France prior to Operation Barbarossa. The vehicle is finished overall in Dunkelgrau RAL 7021, which was introduced as the base color beginning in mid-1940, but too late for the campaigns in the west. The Tac number, white 24, is seen on the both superstructure side plates as well as the rear plate.

StuG.III Ausf.B, StuG.Abt.243, Ostfront, 1941
Established in May, 1941, this unit saw service from the beginning of Operation Barbarossa, with its assault guns painted overall Dunkelgrau RAL 7021. Its insignia consisted of a mounted knight, in white on a red shield, outlined in white. This was typically seen on the casemate side plates. Photographs show various playing card symbols, such as a heart or a diamond behind the knight's head on the shield. These are thought to represent the individual Kompanien within the Abteilung. A white outline Balkenkreuz is also seen on the supplementary casemate side plate. This and the unit insignia are probably repeated on the superstructure's rear plate.

StuG.III Ausf.A, StuG.-Batterie 660, France 1940

This vehicle is finished in a base color of Dunkelgrau Nr.46 (later the code was changed to RAL 7021). This was over-sprayed with Dunkelbraun Nr.45 (later RAL 7017) in patches, so it covered roughly 1/3 of the item being painted. The unit insignia is an open white Maltese Cross, seen on the port side front mud-flap; some vehicles had this insignia on both. A white-outline Balkenkreuz is seen on both sides of the superstructure; this is probably repeated on the rear plate as well.

StuG.III Ausf.A, 4.(Sturmgeschütz) Kompanie bei V.(schweren) Bataillon Leibstandarte Adolf Hitler, Soviet Union, 1941

This assault gun is finished in a single color, Dunkelgrau RAL 7021; it sports a eagle's head with the letters LAH superimposed over it, all in white. This entire emblem is itself is superimposed over a yellow stylized "S", which is believed to represent the name of the unit's commander, SS-Hauptsturmführer Georg Schönberger. A Tac number, 5, in white is seen on the rear superstructure plate, while a black Balkenkreuz outlined in white is seen on the superstructure side plates. Other photographs exist showing vehicles from this unit, at this approximate time, with the plain the white key, or with the key enclosed within a shield, on the rear superstructure plate; this was later adopted as the divisional insignia.

StuG.III Ausf.F, unidentified unit, Ostfront, 1942-43
From March of 1942, the Ausf.F began production; this particular assault gun features factory installed tropical air cleaners and was also painted in the "Tropen" scheme. At its time of production, the colors were Braun RAL 8020 as the base with patches of Grau RAL 7027 covering remaining 1/3 of the item. A standard black/white Balkenkreuz was seen on each armored pannier and was also probably carried on the rear superstructure plate. Where possible, German AFVs destined for use in the southern part of the Soviet Union were outfitted and painted in this manner.

StuG.III Ausf.F, unidentified unit, Ostfront, 1942-43
This assault gun has had a hard-edge winter white camouflage pattern painted over its Dunkelgrau RAL 7021 base color, leaving about one-quarter of the original color visible. No insignia are apparent in the photo upon which this plate is based.

StuG.III Ausf.G, unknown unit time and place, post-February 1943
This assault gun is finished in a base of Dunkelgelb RAL 7028. To this base color was added a camouflage pattern of Olivegrün RAL 6003 and Rotbraun 8017. A three-digit Tac number, possibly 322, was painted in black with a white outline on the hull Schürzen, above a similarly-colored Balkenkreuz.

StuG.III Ausf.G, unknown unit, time and place
Finished overall in Dunkelgelb RAL 7028, this Zimmerit-encrusted assault gun has some rather unique markings on its cast Topfblende mantle, a Tac number, 104, in black with a white outline. A smaller version of the Tac number is painted on the casemate side, forward of the Balkenkreuz national insignia.

StuG.III Ausf.G, unidentified unit, Ostfront, late 1944
In February of 1943, the base color of all new equipment was changed to Dunkelgelb RAL 7028. To this base color could be added a camouflage pattern by using two colors that were issued in a concentrated form for application in the field. These were Olivegrün RAL 6003 and Rotbraun 8017. In the case of this assault gun, it would appear that only a winter whitewash was applied over the plain base color. A Tac number, 02, possibly in red, can be seen just forward of the standard black/white Balkenkreuz on the casemate side. This was likely repeated on the opposite side.

StuG.III Ausf.G, unknown unit, Ostfront, 1944-45
In December of 1944 the base color of all German AFVs was ordered changed to Olivegrün RAL 6003. The remaining two colors, Dunkelgelb RAL 7028 and Rotbraun 8017 would then be applied at the factory. It would appear that this assault gun has been painted in that scheme. A commonly-observed practice was to permanently install segments of the hull Schürzen on the fender and casemate, with the vehicle's Tac number painted on it. In this case it is 133 with a stenciled white edge, filled in with black.

StuG.IV, unidentified unit, possibly France, summer of 1944
This StuG.IV is finished in the base color of Dunkelgelb RAL 7028, with a camouflage pattern consisting of Olivegrün RAL 6003 and Rotbraun 8017 on its body. The hull Schürzen appear to be left un-painted except for the base color; a three-digit Tac number, black 331 outlined in white, appears over a standard black/white Balkenkreuz.

Sturmpanzer IV, unknown unit, place and time
This assault gun is finished overall in Dunkelgelb RAL 7028. A white Tac number, 13, appears on the rear of the superstructure side plate, with a standard black/white Balkenkreuz just ahead and below it. The Sturmpanzer is coated in Zimmerit and mounts a full set of Schürzen.

A schwerer Zugkraftwagen 18-ton (Sd.Kfz.9), anchored by a Sturmgeschütz III Ausf.F/8, attempts to recover a seriously bogged-down Ausf.F/8. The halftrack, also known as the "Bülle" (Bull) was an organic part of the StuG.Abt., and was used as the unit's standard heavy recovery vehicle. Note that both assault guns have been fitted with Schürzen (skirts) to counter the penetrating effects of Soviet man-portable anti-tank rifles on their relatively-thin hull side plates.

The better part of an Infanterie-Zug (infantry platoon) gather around a Sturmgeschütz III Ausf.F/8 to hear the orders of their commander. The assault gun is identified as an Ausf.F/8 by the configuration of the superstructure rear plate and the domed exhaust vent cover on the casemate roof.

In far less-comfortable circumstances, infantrymen gather near a Sturmgeschütz III Ausf.F/8 somewhere on the Ostfront. This assault gun has welded Zusatzpanzer (appliqué armor) plates in the usual locations and the drilled out hull side extensions. It also wears widened Winterketten (winter tracks) for better flotation in the mud and snow that prevailed in this combat zone.

The earliest Sturmgeschütz III Ausf.Gs still retained the two openings over the driver's visor as seen here; note how the 30mm Zusatzpanzer (appliqué armor) plates have a blank space between them in that particular area. Zusatzpanzer has also been bolted to the glacis and bow plate. Note also the rails and Schürzen (skirts) mounted on the assault gun's flanks. This "initial production" Ausf.G also introduced the commander's all around vision cupola, with periscopes, seen here.

This initial production Sturmgeschütz III Ausf.G tows a leichte Gepanzerte Munitionskraftwagen (light armored ammunition transporter) Sd.Kfz.252 through a Soviet city, possibly Kharkov in early 1943. Note the cable passing in-between the two vehicles as well as a second Ausf.G bringing up the rear. The near assault gun is identified as the initial production version by the view-port flap to the left of the driver's station, the angle of the front armor plate on the sponson and the two openings for a periscope over the driver's visor. Note also the new commander's cupola with periscopes to provide all-around vision while closed down.

This Sturmgeschütz III Ausf.G has the features of the more standardized early production version. Of note is a change in the angle to the front plate of the sponson and the hinged shield (seen here folded down) on the roof plate to protect the loader as he manned the external MG34 or MG42. Note how these assault guns have hung spare track lengths on the sponson sides as well as the abundance of stowage items, especially on the engine deck.

Although of relatively poor quality, this image shows a pair of Sturmgeschütz III Ausf.Gs, the nearest of which appears to have concrete blocks placed between its Schürzen (skirts) and the sponson sides. It also appears as if there may be concrete blocks on the glacis plate, above the spare track on the bow. Note that the shield for the loader's MG34 or MG42 is in the raised position.

A soldier (either US or Soviet, judging by his steel helmet) rummages about on the rear deck of a Sturmgeschütz III Ausf.G. From this angle, the rear deck armor plate configuration identifies this as an Ausf.G. Note the Balkenkreuz, which is split between the two plate segments and the white/black Tac number, 233; it appears that some other marking has been obliterated.

The crewmen of these five Sturmgeschütz III Ausf.Gs get acquainted with their new mounts, probably at the Alkett factory. Note the Zimmerit anti-magnetic mine paste, which has been applied in the so-called "Waffle Plate" pattern; this was reputedly a characteristic of this factory. These assault guns feature the cast Topfblende (pot mantle) for the 7.5cm StuK40 L/48 and also have the loader's MG shield in the raised position.

This Sturmgeschütz III Ausf.G has backed itself into a tree-line to better conceal itself from enemy observation; its winter white-wash helps to further hide it. There is an MG34 mounted in the raised loader's shield, and the StuK40 is mounted within a cast Topfblende (pot mantle). The 50mm-thick front plates of the casemate armor feature the typical bolted-on 30mm Zusatzpanzer (appliqué armor) plates, while the bow and glacis feature the 80mm-thick plates introduced during production. Note the Tac number, 02, on the sponson, just forward of the Balkenkreuz.

It is difficult to see the details on this Sturmgeschütz III Ausf.G due to the application of foliage by the crew as a means of concealment, which of course is the reason they did it. However, we can see the cast Topfblende (pot mantle) as well as the remnants of Schürzen (skirts) on the flanks of the assault gun.

Accompanied by infantrymen, this Sturmgeschütz III Ausf.G prepares to move out. Aside from the normal features of its type, which include bolted-on Zusatzpanzer (appliqué armor) plates, MG shield (with MG34 at-the-ready) and welded mantle, other less common items are in evidence. These include the banks of triple-tube Nebelwurfgerät (smoke candle dischargers) on either side of the casemate and Mittelstollen (central grousers) on the faces of the 40cm tracks. The crew has also added thin plates and spare road-wheels on either side of the casemate for added protection.

Waffen-SS infantrymen gather in an anti-tank ditch as a StuG.III Ausf.G begins to cross, in this familiar image. The Sturmgeschütz has several features of interest. These include: Schürzen plates arranged to protect its thinner flanks from Soviet ant-tank rifle fire, an MG34 mounted in the loader's folding gun shield, sunshades on the commander's Scherenfernrohr (scissors periscope) and two rod antennae mounted at the rear corners of the casemate; these last items indicate this is a command vehicle. The two men directly behind the SS man at right appear to be Soviet Red Army prisoners; note their very closely cropped haircuts, perhaps indicating that they are new recruits.

Clutching his MP40, a snow-suited infantryman approaches the rear of a StuG.III Ausf.G, itself already covered with troops. The commander's cupola hatch lid, with an opened flap for his Scherenfernrohr (scissors periscope) identifies this as an Ausf.G. The Sturmgeschütz also wears Schürzen on its flanks as protection against Soviet anti-tank rifles; it is over-painted in a winter whitewash for camouflage against the snow. Note the black/white Balkenkreuz national insignia as well as the gun-in-battery letter, "A", on the rear superstructure plate.

A relatively non-descript pair of Sturmgeschütz III Ausf.G move across the steppes of the Ostfront as German infantrymen (probably Waffen-SS) head in the opposite direction. Both assault guns wear Schürzen (skirts), with the far vehicle having a camouflage pattern applied to the plates.

This detail photograph shows a StuG.III Ausf.G with a concrete-reinforced front superstructure. The 7.5cm StuK40 L/48 has a canvas cover on its muzzle brake and part of the track guard is missing.

This winter-camouflaged Sturmgeschütz III Ausf.G has an interesting combination of features, some early and some later. For instance, the Schürzen (skirts) have the two middle plates divided into upper and lower halves and the loader's station has the fold-down shield for his free-firing MG34 or MG42. Later features include the cast shield welded in front of the commander's cupola, the cast Topfblende (pot mantle) for the StuK40 and the 80mm-thick glacis and bow plates.

Completely oblivious of its surroundings, a local bovine specimen poses for the photographer, tethered to the StuK40 gun tube of a Sturmgeschütz III Ausf.G. This assault gun has bolted-on 30mm-thick Zusatzpanzer (appliqué armor) on the glacis, bow and casemate front plates, as well as the folded-down shield for the loader's MG. There are also triple-tube Nebelwurfgerät (smoke candle dischargers) on either side of the casemate; note that the muzzle brake has been twisted 90-degrees, so that the baffle openings face the sky and the earth.

A group of StuG.III Ausf.Gs advance along a dirt road as columns of smoke rise into the sky behind them. These assault guns are identified as Ausf.Gs by the commander's cupola and the configuration of the superstructure. Note the folded-down shield for the loader's MG, the Schürzen (skirt) plates affixed to the vehicle's flanks, and the sparse vegetation used in an attempt to break up the vehicle's outline.

Posing amidst the destruction brought on by the brutal conflict on the Ostfront, this Sturmgeschütz III Ausf.G has typical features of an assault gun built in 1943. Note the missing bolts on the 30-mm-thick Zusatzpanzer (appliqué armor) fitted over the driver's station; the remaining plates all have the proper pattern and number of bolts. The usual brackets and mounts, with Schürzen (skirt) plates, are affixed to the vehicle's flanks. There is a large un-ditching beam precariously-perching on one side of the assault gun; a close examination of the spare tracks on the bow will reveal that one, possibly two, of the links have solid guide horns.

A StuG.III Ausf.G advances past a burned-out rural building. It features the later cast Topfblende (pot mantle), but the earlier rubber-tired return rollers. In fact, although the cast mantle is normally considered as a "late" feature, the "earlier" mantle, fabricated out of flat plates, was still seen on newly-produced assault guns until the war's end. Also note the long, tube-shaped sun shades over the lenses of the commander's Scherenfernrohr (scissors periscope).

This relatively new StuG.III Ausf.G is helping a Horch 830 up a muddy slope; note the attached tow cable. The Ausf.G is marked as it would have appeared upon issue to a unit, with only the factory-applied Balkenkreuz national insignia in three places: both sides of the casemate and on the rear superstructure plate; there is quite probably a railroad shipping label stenciled on the opposite side of the casemate. This Sturmgeschütz is also outfitted as a command vehicle; note the two 2-meter rod antennae, one at each rear corner of the casemate.

A group of AFV crewmen and Panzergrenadiers receive their orders prior to a mission. The vehicle in the background is a StuG.III Ausf.G as seen by its cast "Topfblende" (pot mantle) and the long StuK40 main gun. The uniforms the men are wearing resemble the standard M1935 items worn by Panzer crewmen, but are the M1940 assault gun crewman's unique version. The two men to the left wear the original collar tabs with death's heads (similar to those worn by the Panzertruppen) that were ordered discontinued at the end of January, 1943. The man at the far right wears the same uniform, but with collar tabs in the more traditional "Guard's Braids" style.

A Sturmgeschütz III Ausf.G provides the background as a group of men belonging to Fallschirm-Panzer-Division "Hermann Göring", converse, perhaps when autumn turned to winter in Italy, 1943. The assault gun wears Schürzen (skirts) on its flanks and features an MG42 mounted in the loader's upright MG shield; it appears that the bow and glacis plate armor is 80mm-thick. Secondary sources indicate that at this time the division had a three-Abtielung organization in Panzer-Regiment "Hermann Göring", with medium tanks in two of them and assault guns forming the third.

What is apparently a Soviet soldier, crawls towards a StuG.III Ausf.G whose commander has his "head out" of his cupola to better observe the enemy; note the Scherenfernrohr (scissors periscope) for long range observation just in front of him. This Ausf.G has 30mm Zusatzpanzerung (appliqué armor) bolted to the base of 50mm plates on the hull, glacis and superstructure front. It is outfitted as a command vehicle; note the two 2-meter rod antennae, one at each rear corner of the casemate. This Ausf.G also has the first style of framing, without the triangle-shaped hooks, for hanging Schürzen (skirt) plates.)

Well hidden in lush, mountainous terrain, the commander of a Sturmgeschütz III Ausf.G observes possible enemy movements through his binoculars. The commander's cupola with its periscopes is easily visible, as is the lens of the gunner's Sfl.Z.F.1a sighting periscope. This assault gun has 30mm Zusatzpanzer (appliqué armor) plates bolted over the driver's compartment's base of 50mm; the glacis and bow plates appear to be 80mm-thick.

As a German soldier digs-in, he is caught by the photographer, who used a Sturmgeschütz III Ausf.G as a background; it seems the man in the middle-ground may also be a photographer. This indicates a Propaganda-Kompanie unit is in the area. The assault gun has the remnant of a Schürzen (skirts) plate on its near flank, above the track-guard. Note the Tac number, 113, forward of the Balkenkreuz, on the plate itself, the long un-ditching log below the plate, and the spare track behind it.

This pair of Sturmgeschütz III Ausf.Gs lie in wait behind the crest of a low ridge; there appears to be a Marder-type Panzerjäger at far left covering that particular flank. The assault guns are rather common in their appearance, with only Balkenkreuze national insignia in various places on their winter white-washed bodies. Note that the near assault gun has two antennae (indicating it is a command vehicle) on the rear of the casemate and that it also has a tow hitch hanging from the center of the hull rear plate.

A train-load of StuG.III Ausf.Gs, from SS-Division "Das Reich" makes their way to the front. The Ausf.G introduced a circular commander's cupola with periscopes around the rim and a hatch lid that rotated and could be partially opened in front for the commander's "Scherenfernrohr" (scissors periscope). The Ausf.G also introduced a completely re-designed superstructure, which did away with the separate radio panniers, moved the housing for the fighting compartment fume extractor fan to the rear plate (the first 120 had it on the roof, but without the raised section as seen on the Ausf.F and F/8) and introduced a new loader's hatch design. Later versions also had a hinged shield in front of the loader's hatch so he could fire an MG34 or MG42 with some protection from enemy fire. Most of these features can be seen on the first assault gun at the bottom of the photo. Note that it does not have 30mm plates bolted to the glacis and hull front plates, but that the next assault gun in line does; this one also has the triple-tube Nebelwurfgerät (smoke candle discharger) fitted to the superstructure sides. The markings on the hull are the temporary markings used at Kursk by SS-Division "Das Reich", while the playing card symbols probably denote the battery within SS-Sturmgeschütz-Abtielung 2. Most photographs that show German AFVs on trains do not exhibit chains holding the vehicles in place; unusually, this photo does, as can be seen on the first vehicle.

While the apparently jovial commander of this Sturmgeschütz III Ausf.G looks on, his driver maneuvers the assault gun through the brick columns of a gated area. The hull configuration indicates that it has 80mm-thick plates on the bow and glacis plates; the remainder of the frontal arc has bolted 30-mm Zusatzpanzer (appliqué armor) plates.

This remarkable photograph depicts at least 20 brand-new Sturmgeschütz III Ausf.Gs as they await shipment (probably at the Alkett plant) to the rail-head for their journey to the front. Note the Panther Ausf.A in the middle and the columns of newly-produced Hummel 15cm s.FH18-armed self-propelled howitzers. The assault guns are all covered with a tailored tarp to keep the elements at bay; note also the brackets for the racks to mount Schürzen (skirts) laying on several engine decks. Both welded and cast Topfblende (pot mantles) are in evidence on the StuK40 main armament.

Infantrymen take shelter in a drainage ditch beside a road, as a VW Typ82 Kübelwagen overtakes a Sturmgeschütz III Ausf.G. The assault gun is based on a hull with 80mm-thick armor on the glacis and bow, with bolted-on 30mm-thick Zusatzpanzer (appliqué armor) plates on the casemate front. It has a slab-sided, welded mantle for the StuK40 and the Schürzen (skirts) are attached directly to the track guard.

Laden with a large amount of spare track for added protection, this Sturmgeschütz III Ausf.G leads a column of Italian-built medium tanks; the latter are probably M14/41s or M15/42s, all based on the earlier M13/40 design. At a certain point during production, the Ausf.G was fitted with an external Heckzurrung (travel lock) for the main gun, as seen here.

This MIAG-built Sturmgeschütz III Ausf.G is identified as such by the "cross-hatch" pattern of the Zimmerit anti-magnetic mine paste. It has a high wooden parapet added to its rear deck and also mounts two rod antennae, indicating its possible role as a command vehicle. Note the distinct camouflage pattern on the Schürzen (skirts), the dismounted Notek black-out driving head-lamp and the "C"-shaped tow hooks in the ready-use position at the bow.

While some German infantrymen loiter, another group boards a Sturmgeschütz III Ausf.G. Note that the Schürzen (skirts) have a Tac number and a Balkenkreuz on the third plate. The assault gun carries an un-ditching log on its near side and the crew has already deployed their pair of "C"-shaped tow hooks for rapid recovery under fire.

This destroyed StuG.III Ausf.G has had much of its suspension blown away, as well as the roof plate, making it very likely that it is not salvageable. It has a later cast Topfblende (pot mantle). It also has the so-called "waffle-plate" pattern Zimmerit, which was a characteristic of the Alkett factory; note how it is also applied to the lower side of the hull. There is a single Balkenkreuz applied to the superstructure side, which is covered in a base color of Dunkelgelb; any other colors are hidden under dust or stains from battle damage.

While troops seek cover on its rear deck, this StuG.III Ausf.G fires its main gun at the enemy. Note the storage of the engine starter crank on the rear plate, the standard stowage of two spare road-wheels on each of the rear-most engine ventilation cowls, as well as the erected MG shield on the superstructure roof.

This Sturmgeschütz III Ausf.G has an unusual hull configuration, in that the 30-mm-thick Zusatzpanzer (appliqué armor) has been welded (instead of being bolted) on to the glacis and bow plates. This image also excellently illustrates how the commander's cupola hatch lid could rotate; note its position and the opened flap for the use of the Scherenfernrohr" (scissors periscope); when mounted, it allowed the commander to observe the enemy from under armor. Notable stowage items include road-wheels on either track guard and two separate strands of spare track of the solid guide horn type (each set faces a different direction) on the bow plate. Other typical features are the fitting of Schürzen (skirt) plates and their suspension system, as well as the raised shield for the loader's MG34 machine-gun.

Parked in front of a protective shed, this Sturmgeschütz III Ausf.G exhibits several of its identifying features. In particular, the commander's cupola and the 80mm-thick glacis and bow plate are visible, as are the rails and plates for the Schürzen (skirts) on its flanks. Note the Jagdpanzer 38 parked at left in the photo; this vehicle was designed as a direct result of an Allied bombing raid, which severely disrupted the production of the Sturmgeschütz III Ausf.G.

Bulgaria received 55 Sturmgeschütz III Ausf.Gs, which they designated "Maybach T-III". These vehicles, one of which is seen here climbing a small rise, equipped the 1st Assault Gun Battalion. Note the uniforms on the visible crewmen, which, although they have a "German" appearance, are a bit different, especially in the head-gear. This Ausf.G is built on a later hull with the single 80mm plates on the glacis and bow; note the "ready-for-use" tow cable attached by a tow hook to the drilled hull-side extensions. Very prominent in this photograph is the Notek black-out driving head-lamp and its mounting bracket, situated on the center of the glacis plate.

This Bulgarian Maybach T-III (Sturmgeschütz III Ausf.G) has some subtle but unusual features, which will reveal themselves to the sharp-eyed observer. For instance, it would appear that the glacis and bow plates are of 80mm thickness. Note also that the starboard-side casemate front plate has bolted-on 30mm Zusatzpanzerung (appliqué armor) plates. The port-side superstructure plate always had the bolted-on armor, since it had to be based on a 50mm plate. This was because the driver's visor was the Fahrersehklappe 50, which could only be used on a plate of that thickness. This Ausf.G has three other notable details. The first is the cast armor shield welded in front of the commander's cupola, the second is the position of the MG34 on the loader's folding shield; it is in the upper-most mount for use against aircraft. The third is the cast Topfblende (pot handle) gun mantle. Finally note the Bulgarian registration plate on the starboard-side superstructure plate; the numbers in this series ranged from B60501 to B60555.

This Maybach T-III (Sturmgeschütz III Ausf.G) shows the more typical style of vehicle registration plate, featuring black characters on a white rectangle with a black border; in this case the number is B60537. This Ausf.G features the cast armor shield welded in front of the commander's cupola, the loader's folding shield with the MG34 protruding through an opening (note the extended bipod) and the cast Topfblende (pot handle) gun mantle. The hull appears to be based on 50mm of armor plate without the bolted-on 30mm Zusatzpanzerung (appliqué armor). Note the stowage of 20-liter jerry cans on both sides of the superstructure, on the fenders, with the mounting rails for the Schürzen holding them in place. It also seems that this is a command vehicle as there are rod antennae on both sides of the rear superstructure plate.

While the driver of this Sturmgeschütz III Ausf.G pilots his assault gun, the remaining crewmen receive the cheers of passers-by as they make their way through a town. This assault gun features the Zimmerit pattern associated with the MIAG factory, and also has the welded mantle for the StuK40; the author has not seen a photograph with this Zimmerit pattern in combination with a cast Topfblende (pot mantle). Note also the 80mm-thick bow and glacis plates as well as the mounting rails and plates for the Schürzen (skirts).

This jaunty Leutnant poses on his Sturmgeschütz III Ausf.G after receiving his Ritterkreuz (Knight's Cross). There are 40 kill rings on the StuK40, which appears to be topped by a new muzzle brake in a much darker color than the remainder of the gun. The Notek black-out driving head-lamp is clearly visible, as are the bolts holding the 30mm-thick Zusatzpanzer (appliqué armor) in place.

A pair of early Sturmgeschütz III Ausf.Gs passes warily through a Soviet village or collective farm. The angle of the sun pops out the bolt-head details of the bow and glacis-mounted 30mm-thick Zusatzpanzer (appliqué armor). Both assault guns are buttoned-up, with not even the commander's daring to expose themselves; this indicates the anticipation of combat at any time.

The crew of this Waffen-SS StuG.III Ausf.G appear to be busying themselves with the erection of a canvas cover over their gun. The commander, shown in his cupola, wears the trademark Russian fur "Ushanka" cap and has the Waffen-SS eagle on his sleeve, while the man at far left wears a great-coat with the unusual addition of collar tabs. This Ausf.G is identified as such by the commander's cupola; note also that the crew have trimmed back the sharp upper and lower edges of the front and rear plates of their early-style Schürzen in an attempt to minimize the risk of their snagging on something and being torn off.

In the company of an Opel 3-ton truck, this Sturmgeschütz III Ausf.G passes a grain silo or water tower. The assault gun is fitted with 30mm-thick Zusatzpanzer (appliqué armor) on the bow, glacis and casemate front. The crew has also placed a canvas cover over the front end of the casemate in order to keep out dust, rain and cold temperatures; the front-end of this vehicle was quite "leaky". The StuK40 is fixed to the internal travel lock and has a canvas bag covering the muzzle brake; this indicates that combat is not immediately expected.

These three StuG.III Ausf.Gs take up positions on the open steppes, while their crewmen have a look around. While the farthest assault gun has its flanks shielded by Schürzen (skirts), the other two do not; there are no rails attached either. Note the use of spare track as added protection on two of them, as well as the ever-present rear deck stowage. The near Sturmgeschütz has the loader's MG34 mounted in place behind his folding gun shield.

This later production version StuG.III Ausf.G has suffered an explosion massive enough to rip its roof completely from the casemate. Note the non-standard way in which the Schürzen were mounted and the Tac number, 100, over a Balkenkreuz national insignia on the remaining plate. The drive sprocket is the type seen on later assault guns that had no hub cap to cover the final drive attachment bolts, and the return rollers are one variation of the later all-steel types; this kind has six spokes on a plain disk.

An American soldier poses for a photo while sitting on the track guard of a Sturmgeschütz III Ausf.G, possibly in Italy. At a certain point in time, many of these assault guns featured drive sprockets without an armored cover over the hub bolts, as seen here. This Ausf.G also features the cast Topfblende (pot mantle) for the StuK40, as well as the cast shield in front of the commander's cupola; it also features the Zimmerit pattern associated with the Alkett factory.

A pair of US soldiers rummage through a captured Sturmgeschütz III Ausf.G, which exhibits some later production features. These include 80mm-thick plates on the bow and glacis, as well as an 80mm plate on the starboard front of the casemate. The 30mm-thick plate at the port side, which was bolted in place was used until the end of production. This was because the driver's armored visor was designed to be installed in a plate 50mm-thick, and was never re-designed to fit in a plate 80mm-thick. The assault gun has a waffle pattern application of Zimmerit, typical of the Alkett factory. Note the Schürzen (skirts) and cast Topfblende (pot mantle) for the StuK40, as well as the MG34 and MG42s leaning against the bow plate.

As an M2A1 or M3A1 armored half-track rolls by, a US infantryman takes a moment to consider an abandoned Sturmgeschütz III Ausf.G, which exhibits some later production features. These include drive sprocket without hub-cap, perforated all-steel return rollers (note that the center one is missing) and cast shield welded in front of the commander's cupola. Note also the twisted remains of the hanging rail for Schürzen (skirts) on the near side of this assault gun.

This Sturmgeschütz III Ausf.G exhibits many of the earlier features, particularly bolted-on 30mm-thick Zusatzpanzer (appliqué armor) on the glacis and casemate front plates; although obscured by foliage and spare track, it is quite probable that a plate has also been bolted on to the bow. This assault gun has the welded mantle for the StuK40 and also has what appears to be a full set of Schürzen (skirts) on both flanks. Note the three-tone camouflage scheme and the Balkenkreuz on the Schürzen.

Possibly the most unusual items seen in this oft-published image depict constructs of Soviet origin. Note the rare appearance of a "surfaced" highway, being joined by the more usual (in this case quite dusty!) dirt track. The T-34s in the foreground both have a cast turret mounting the 76.2mm F-34 main gun; this type of turret/hull combination was produced until the spring of 1943 at Factory 112, and until the early months of 1942 at Factory 183. The Sturmgeschütz III Ausf.G has the usual features seen on those produced in early 1943 to include bolted-on 30mm-thick Zusatzpanzer (appliqué armor) and Schürzen (skirts) on both flanks. This assault gun also has road-wheels stored low on the rear superstructure plate and carries two antennae, indicating that it is a command vehicle.

In what is quite probably a "true" combat photograph, a Sturmgeschütz III Ausf.G moves forward under enemy fire; note the remnant of a recent explosion, far left. The crew has modified the Schürzen (skirts) by attaching some plates directly to the track guards, and leaning others in towards the casemate side walls. There is also a Tac number and Balkenkreuz painted on the upper plate sections.

This Sturmgeschütz III Ausf.G exhibits some, but not all of the later production features. It appears to have 80-mm thick glacis and bow plates and a close look reveals that this is possibly the case for the casemate front, on the starboard side. Note the configuration of the muzzle brake and the use of a cast Topfblende (pot mantle) on the long StuK40 main gun. A full set of Schürzen (skirts) protects each flank of this assault gun.

A column of five Sturmgeschütz III Ausf.Gs pause along a dusty road followed by a Volkswagen Typ166 Schwimmwagen light amphibious car. Of interest is that the second and fifth Ausf.Gs are based on the Pz.Kpfw.III Ausf.M chassis, which was optimized for deep wading; note the unique exhaust mufflers at the rear ends of each of these two assault guns. These assault guns all have stowage on their rear superstructure plates consisting of such things as helmets and water bottles, while most have a short section of spare track stored rolled around the spare road-wheels on the engine deck. The earlier pattern Schürzen plates are fitted to what are otherwise rather mundane-looking vehicles.

A rare sight, these SS-Fallschirmjäger (note helmet and eagle on left sleeve) have dug in their MG42, with a Sturmgeschütz III Ausf.G in support. Secondary sources indicate the Waffen-SS had at least two parachute-trained units, SS-Fallschirmjäger-Bataillon 500 and 600; these units saw notable action in Italy, the Balkans and during the Ardennes Offensive. The assault gun has the remains of the mounting frames for Schürzen (skirts) on its near side, and mounts ribbed all-steel return rollers.

A Sturmgeschütz III Ausf.G parks itself on the main street of a town, probably on the western front in 1944. It is identified as an Ausf.G by the commander's cupola with periscopes; along with this improvement came an entirely re-designed casemate and roof layout. This Ausf.G has foliage and some sort of camouflage mesh or netting draped around its flanks, reflecting the crew's concern that should the need arise, they can be quickly shielded from the watchful eyes of roving Allied Air Forces' "Jabo" (fighter-bomber) pilots.

This later StuG.III Ausf.G has a number of interesting features. It is fitted with the wider "Ostketten" (east tracks) on its running gear and also has these as spare track sections on the superstructure front angled plates. It has 80mm armor as a basis; note the upper and lower glacis plates as well as the lack of bolts on the single 80mm plate on the starboard side of the superstructure front. A Heckzurrung (external travel lock) is fitted next to the Notek head-lamp, while the gun itself is housed in a cast Topfblende (pot mantle). Note the improvised gun shield around the loader's MG; at first glance it would appear to be the standardized Rundumfeuer (360-degree traverse MG mount). However, it more closely resembles the MG shield commonly seen on German armored half-tracks.

This destroyed Sturmgeschütz III Ausf.G has several late-production features. Note the perforated all-steel return rollers, stowage frame on the engine deck and drive sprocket without hub cap. It also has the cast shield in front of the commander's cupola as well as a cast Topfblende (pot mantle) for the StuK40. Produced sometime after September 1944, it has not been coated with Zimmerit, which was officially discontinued in that month.

It is likely that this Sturmgeschütz III Ausf.G was demolished by its own crew after becoming bogged down near this river; why any one would be compelled to enter such a place is indeed a mystery. Note that the casemate roof plate is nowhere to be seen, as well as the twisted remains of a stowage rack on the engine deck. This assault gun has been fitted with the welded mantle for the StuK40.

This Sturmgeschütz III Ausf.G has seen better days; note the track that has been blown away from the far drive sprocket and the bent steel strip that normally held spare track links, spanning the bow plate. This assault gun has a welded mantle for the StuK40 and a cast shield welded to the front of the commander's cupola. Note also the interesting bin on the side of the casemate, filled with road-wheels; this is reminiscent of the type seen on the Pz.Kpfw.IV and StuG.IV.

Although of lesser quality, this image depicts a Sturmgeschütz III Ausf.G mounting a 10.5cm l.FH18, which makes it a Sturmhaubitze 42. This vehicle has the muzzle brake typically seen on the towed field howitzer, not the larger flanged type, or the double-baffle type that resembles an enlarged StuK40 muzzle brake. This is a later vehicle as can be seen by the loader's hatch configuration, the mount for the Rundumfeuer (360-degree traverse MG mount) and the perforated all-steel return rollers.

This Sturmgeschütz III Ausf.G with the Alkett "waffle plate" Zimmerit pattern exhibits some unique features. Most prominent is the addition of the armored cowls that normally cover the openings in the engine deck hatch lids, to the glacis plate. A close look will also reveal parts of the foundry numbers on the cast Topfblende (pot-handle) gun mantle. Aside from the frames and brackets to mount Schürzen, this crew has also added lengths of spare track on nearly every vertical surface that can be seen. Note the Balkenkreuz painted on a plate that covers some spare track on the casemate side.

At first glance this Sturmgeschütz III Ausf.G appears to be relatively standard, until one notes the short, thick gun tube; it is actually a Sturmhaubitze 42 mounting a 10.5cm StuH42. Other details of this relatively new assault howitzer include tool stowage, Schürzen (skirts) and their mounting frame, rod antenna with base, and crew stowage on the rear wall of the casemate. The commander's Scherenfernrohr (scissors periscope) are also visible, protruding from his opened cupola hatch.

A train loaded with Sturmgeschütz III Ausf.Gs is seen in a rail-yard. Beginning with the fragment of the Ausf.G in the immediate foreground, take note of the "cross-hatch" MIAG factory Zimmerit pattern, which is barely seen on the forward-most edge of the superstructure front plate. This assault gun also has the welded slab-sided gun mantle as can be seen by the gun tube's sleeve with its slotted fastening screws. The vehicles on the rail cars have late all-steel return rollers with six reinforcing ribs, as well as the drive sprocket without the hub cap to protect the rim bolts. There are rails for Schürzen on each, with the plates themselves seen stored on the engine deck so the overall vehicle width would conform to rail-road shipping width limitations. No safety chains are in evidence to secure these AFVs to the rail cars; holding them in place are only wooden wedges fore and aft (and probably on the platform inside the track runs to prevent lateral shifting).

A group of Soviet Red Army soldiers stand atop and around their American-made Studebaker US-6 2.5-ton tactical truck, while a destroyed Sturmgeschütz III Ausf.G completes the picture. The assault gun has concrete armor on the front of the casemate and has other late-production features, such as 80mm-thick bow and glacis plates, all-steel return rollers and no hub cap on the drive sprocket. Note the plate affixed to a frame over the track guards; this features a Tac number, 133.

This Alkett-produced Sturmgeschütz III Ausf.G (note the "waffle plate" Zimmerit pattern) has seen better days. It is uniquely-marked with a Tac number, 104, on the cast Topfblende (pot-handle) gun mantle; this is repeated on the casemate side where Zimmeret has been removed. Note also that the crew has added concrete armor between the casemate side wall and the commander's cupola.

This Sturmgeschütz III Ausf.G exhibits most of the features that would be seen on the final production versions of this particular model. They include: MG34 in the Rundumfeuer (360-degree traverse MG mount), Topfblende (cast, pot-shaped gun mantle) with co-axial MG34, and Heckzurrung (external travel lock for gun) on the glacis. There is a cast shield welded in front of the commander's cupola and this vehicle would also have had the Nahverteidigungswaffe (close defense weapon) or a covering plate located on the casemate roof, near the MG mount. Other details to be noted are the missing Notek black-out driving head-lamp (its empty mounting bracket is next to the Heckzurrung on the glacis), the positions of the two "C"-shaped tow hooks on both forward edges of the hull side plates, and the small hinged flap (unseen) on the commander's cupola hatch lid; this opened separately so a Scherenfernrohr (scissors periscope) for long range observation could be used from under cover.

At Hitler's insistence, a number of Sturminfanteriegeschütze were created in haste for the urban fighting in Stalingrad. Of the first 12 converted, six each were sent to StuG.Abt.177 and StuG.Abt.244, to be deployed at Stalingrad as soon as it could be arranged. The chassis of vehicles returned for overhaul were used along with the standard 15cm s.IG33 (heavy infantry gun), mounted within a box-like casemate with a maximum of 80mm of armor. This particular vehicle was captured intact by the Soviets and today resides in Moscow's Kubinka collection. Note the Mittelstollen (center grousers) on the 40cm tracks.

A Sturmgeschütz IV sits destroyed on flooded ground next to its stable mate, a Sturmgeschütz III Ausf.G. The StuG.IV has all-steel return rollers as well as the Topfblende (cast, pot-shaped gun mantle), both of which were common to this assault gun; no photos have been seen to date of the earlier welded, slab-sided mantle on this type. The StuG.III has the modified mounting for its Schürzen, while the StuG.IV has the later style mounting rail with triangle-shaped hooks. Note also that the tray to carry two spare road-wheels is mounted a short distance above the track guard; this was standard practice and not the result of the explosion that destroyed this assault gun.

This fully-equipped, if slightly battered Sturmgeschütz IV moves down a dirt road in the company of a heavy motorcycle combination and several other assault guns. This assault gun mounts the loader's MG42 behind a folding shield. Other points of interest are the un-covered Bosch black-out driving head-lamp and the Tac number, 331, on the Schürzen (skirt), above the Balkenkreuz national insignia.

This group of Sturmgeschütz IVs have typical features for this type, to include: cast Topfblende (pot handle) gun mantle, cast armor shield welded in front of the commander's cupola, and folding shield for the loader's MG. One other detail is a diagonal strip welded to the sloped front of the casemate, just behind the driver's hatch; this was to divert rain water away from the hatch opening.

This gutted Sturmgeschütz IV is examined by an American soldier, probably during the battles in Normandy. The fielding of this particular assault gun came about as a result of Allied bombing raids, which in November 1943 severely disrupted production at Alkett of the highly-prized Sturmgeschütz III. A quickly-designed substitute was composed of a hybrid vehicle mounting the Alkett StuG.III Ausf.G casemates to Krupp Pz.Kpfw.IV Ausf.H and J chassis, the result being the StuG.IV as seen here. Note the extended driver's compartment hood and the plate beside it that filled the space on the Pz.Kpfw.IV hull, since the casemate was mounted back against the original engine compartment firewall. This assault gun wears a coat of Zimmerit in a typical ridged pattern, and very likely belonged to the 17.SS-Panzergrenadier-Division Gotz von Berlichingen.

This destroyed early-production Sturmgeschütz IV is fitted with a Heckzurrung (external travel lock), which can be seen laying in the opening created when the transmission access panel was blown off. This assault gun has Zimmerit anti-magnetic mine paste applied and mounts the StuK40 in a cast Topfblende (pot mantle). Other details include the folding shield for the loader's MG, a cast shield welded in front of the commander's cupola, a spare road-wheel rack on the elevated superstructure side (not on the trackguard itself as would be normal for a Pz.Kpfw.IV chassis), four (instead of the later three) return rollers and the cast idler wheel. It has an extensive array of spare track affixed to its forward surfaces as added protection against enemy fire.

This photo depicts a unit commander's Sturmgeschütz IV (note two radio antennae) as he signals his column. It shows many of this vehicle's features to great advantage such as: commander's cupola with a cast shield welded in front of it, folding MG shield for the loader (with what appears to be an MG42 mounted), cast Topfblende (pot mantle) for the StuK40, driver's position extension with hatch lid and periscope covers, Zimmerit anti-magnetic mine paste, Schürzen (skirt) mounting rails, and spare road-wheel storage tray mounted above the track guards.

A line of new Sturmgeschütz IVs halts on the side of a road. Note that they have Zimmeritt anti-magnetic mine paste and are finished in a monochrome base of Dunkelgelb. There is a black/white Balkenkreuz on the driver's compartment side. Features to note are the cast Topfblende (pot handle) gun mantle, cast armor shield welded forward of the commander's cupola, and the rain gutter just behind the driver's hatch. Note also the tool, spare road-wheel and track storage, as well as the mounting rails for Schürzen (skirts).

This photograph of the roof of a Sturmgeschütz IV reveals several very interesting details. It is indeed a StuG.IV as can be seen by the extended driver's station, with the driver himself occupying the open hatch; the small bit of armored cowl that's visible over the air cooling vents for the brakes can also just be seen to the right of the cast Topfblende (pot handle) gun mantle. Note the deployed MG42 on the roof plate; it rests over the empty mount for the remote-controlled Rundumfeuer (360-degree traverse MG mount). The final items to note are the raised bolts that hold the casemate roof in place and the square plate over the opening for the never-installed Nahverteidigungswaffe (close defense weapon).

Three of the four men assigned as the crew of this Sturmgeschütz IV pose for the photographer, obviously in a warm climate, possibly in Italy. Note the different types of spare track (open and solid guide horns) on the bow and glacis plates as well as the "L"-shaped hooks that were part of the mounting system for Schürzen (skirts).

This knocked-out Sturmgeschütz IV was of a later production series as can be seen from the way the loader's roof hatch lids open to each side; this indicates that a mounting plate for the remote-controlled Rundumfeuer (360-degree traverse MG mount) has been installed. As there were always shortages of this item, it can not be said that this assault gun was ever fitted with one. Other items of note are the non-standard position of the stowed pair of "C"-shaped tow hooks and the four all-steel return rollers.

Probably photographed on the Ostfront during the first months of 1945, this Sturmgeschütz IV exhibits one very interesting feature: the mounting of the MG34 in the remote-controlled Rundumfeuer (360-degree traverse MG mount) on the casemate roof; this was not often seen on these vehicles. This damaged assault gun (note the drive sprocket on the hull) has been daubed with a random white-wash pattern over its camouflage base color; the troops nearby are armed with the MG42 general-purpose machine-gun and StG44 assault rifle.

The first production series of Sturmpanzer IVs can be identified by the driver's armored visor, which was sourced from the Tiger I. Other detail items include the covered Bosch black-out driving head-lamp on the track guard and the gunner's Sfl.Z.F.1a sight projecting from a slit in the casemate roof. This photograph was reputedly taken in Italy, where Stu.Pz.Abt.216 was sent in February 1944 to help defeat the Allied landings at Anzio.

The next production batch of Sturmpanzer IVs dispensed with the armored driver's visor from the Tiger I, and instead, as seen here, was fitted with a periscope and armored guard. This assault gun is fitted with the drive sprocket introduced on the Pz.Kpfw.IV Ausf.H, which was part of the reinforced final drive system. Note also the all-steel return rollers and the Zimmerit anti-magnetic mine paste with its ridged pattern.

Another example of the second production batch of Sturmpanzer IVs is shown here, minus the casemate's roof plate. This assault gun has suspension components from the Pz.Kpfw.IV Ausf.H and J to include: later drive sprocket for reinforced final drive, four all-steel return rollers and cast idler wheel. While the latter is considered a "late" production feature, this idler wheel design was actually superceded on many final Pz.Kpfw.IV derivatives by the previously-used welded tube design. Note the details of the casemate roof plate laying in the foreground; these include the sliding shutter over the gunner's sight aperture as well as the lifting hooks that were used to remove the roof for maintenance or replacement of the 15cm StuH43 main armament.

This photograph reveals the details of a factory-fresh Sturmpanzer IV of the second production batch; it too is based on a Pz.Kpfw.IV Ausf.H or Ausf.J chassis. The vehicle is fully stowed, wears a coat of Zimmerit anti-magnetic mine paste and has a full set of Schürzen (skirts) fitted. Note the canvas cover over the casemate roof, the gun mantle and the gun tube. The Tac number, a solid white "13" is seen on the rear of the casemate, above and behind the Balkenkreuz national insignia.

This final version of the Sturmpanzer IV für 15cm Sturmhaubitze 43 (Sd.Kfz.166) Ausf.IV (Serie IV), lies derelict, stripped of its final drive, its associated drive sprocket and its tracks. The features that clearly identify it as the final type are the single-plate casemate sides (the entire structure was re-designed), the MG34 ball mount above the driver's station, the commander's cupola on the casemate roof and the Gummigefederten Stahllaufrollen (rubber-cushioned steel-tired road-wheels) on the first two bogie units. Several other interesting details are visible in this photo. The commander's cupola has an extendible Fliegerbeschußgerät (anti-aircraft mount for an MG), there are MP-Stopfen (pistol ports) on the casemate sides, late-pattern Schürzen (skirt) rails and their associated fender extensions, and finally, all-steel return rollers. Another Sturmpanzer IV lies abandoned in the background.

US soldiers examine a damaged and abandoned Panzersturmmörser from Sturmmörser-Kompanie 1000, during February of 1945. Note several unique features of this vehicle, including the huge diameter of the bore of the 38cm RW61 mortar (with exhaust gas ports located around the muzzle's rim), the external ammunition hoist (there was also one fitted to the inside roof plate of the fighting compartment), and the stubs on the rim of the mortar's muzzle. These last items were used to mount a large muzzle counter-weight, which could be seen in at least two variations. This Tiger-Mörser also has a Bosch black-out driving head-lamp on the glacis plate and is partially covered in Zimmerit anti-magnetic mine paste; note the MP-Stopfen (pistol port) plug hanging loose on its retaining chain on the casemate's side wall.